How it is made

Glass

Text   Alan J. Paterson
Design   Arthur Lockwood

Contents

faber and faber in association with Threshold Books

The use of glass in modern architecture can be very dramatic, as in these glass-walled buildings.

What is glass?

Take a walk down any street, and you will see people looking in shop windows, carrying bottles, peering through their car windscreens, and wearing spectacles. It won't take you long to find that glass is an essential part of our way of life.

This is not surprising when you consider all that it has to offer. It is transparent. It can be easily shaped. It will not rot, rust, or taint food stuffs. It can be cleaned very easily. It can be recycled (melted and used again). Above all, it is relatively cheap.

What you may not know is that it is a liquid. This may seem strange, as when you pick up a piece it does not run through your fingers like water. Yet it is regarded as a liquid rather than a solid, because when the raw materials are melted together and then cooled, the glass does not become crystalline (the small particles which make up the glass do not form crystals). It is therefore known as a 'supercooled liquid'.

The main ingredient for glassmaking is **silica**. When subjected to powerful heat, silica melts, and on cooling it forms glass. On its own, however, silica is no good for making ordinary glass. Because it needs to reach such a high temperature before it melts – and therefore uses up a considerable amount of energy – it is too expensive. To overcome this problem, substances called **fluxes** are added, to make it melt at lower temperatures. The most common fluxes in use today are soda ash (sodium oxide) and lime (calcium oxide). Mixed raw materials (which are called a **batch**) are melted in a furnace at around $1500°C$ ($3020°F$), along with 'cullet', which is glass either recycled or discarded from the production process.

The first man-made glass appeared in the Eastern Mediterranean area before 3000 BC. It is believed that it was discovered by the Mesopotamians or Egyptians, who used coloured glazes on pottery or stones to make them look like precious or semi-precious gems.

The earliest existing glass vessels date from the Egyptian 18th Dynasty (1500 BC). The earliest glass furnace was found at Tell el Amarna in Egypt, and dates from 1350 BC.

This ship-in-a-bottle was made by a lampworker (see page 27). Fine strands of glass were used for the rigging, and the sails were sand-blasted to make them opaque. The ship was first inserted into a glass cylinder which has one end sealed. Then with remarkable skill the glass worker closes the other end by creating a neck into which he inserts a glass stopper. He has to heat the glass of the bottle without causing damage to the ship inside.

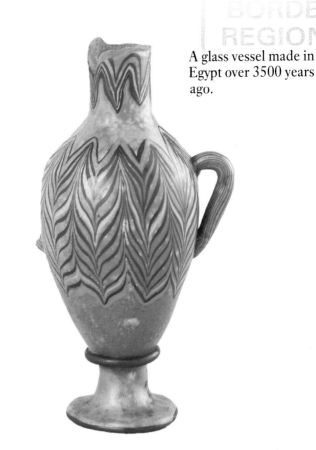

A glass vessel made in Egypt over 3500 years ago.

Types of glass

Because of the many different ways in which it is used, glass has to withstand a variety of conditions. The glass from which a casserole dish is made must be able to withstand the heat of an oven. The glass used for car windscreens must be able to withstand both hot and cold weather, as well as the shock of stones which may be thrown up from the road. The glass for camera lenses must be of a very high quality. To produce each of these types of glass a particular mixture of materials is melted together. The many thousands of types of glass can be divided into three main groups.

Soda-lime-silica glass

This is produced in larger quantities than other types, and its uses are wide and varied – ranging from ashtrays to windows. The combination of silica-sand, soda-ash and limestone produces a glass that is easily melted and shaped. The raw materials are readily available, and therefore it is cheap to produce. It is particularly suited to automatic methods of 'forming', or making.

Its natural colour tends to be greenish, owing to the iron content of the sand. The colour can be corrected by mixing a very small amount of selenium or manganese with the other raw materials.

Lead

This type of glass is made from silica-sand, potash and lead oxide. It has an extremely fine lustre and brilliance, and when expertly cut it gleams and sparkles like a diamond.

The amount of lead in the batch may vary considerably – even up to 92 per cent lead oxide.

Because of the quality of the raw materials it is relatively expensive to produce. Great care is taken in melting, to avoid bubbles in the glass.

Borosilicate

This is made from a combination of silica-sand and boric oxide. *Pyrex*, the well-known ovenware, is a borosilicate glass, which is durable enough not to crack when cold water is poured on to it while it is still hot. This glass can stand up to the demands of industrial and domestic use.

Other types of glass

The three main headings above cover the types of glass which are most commonly used. However, glass can be 'tailor-made' for other purposes. By adding various fluxing agents, the melting point can be raised or lowered; the glass can be strengthened; or it can be made more 'runny' for forming. The runnier it is the more easily it flows into shape.

Feeding the mixture of raw materials which is used for hand-made glass, into a furnace. The mixture can be seen in the large trough in the foreground.

This 18th-century engraving shows a pot furnace with glassblowers at work.

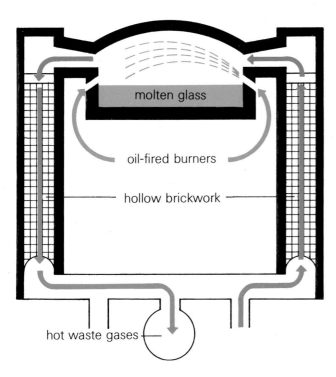

A cross-section of a tank furnace (see pages 10/11). Oil-fired burners melt the glass. To obtain maximum heat from the fuel the hot waste gases from the furnace pass through one of two chambers filled with hollow brickwork (**regenerators**). The bricks act like storage heaters, and when the flow is reversed the heat helps to burn the oil.

Furnaces

Batch mixing
An important part of the glass production process is the mixing of the 'batch'. The basic constituents and additives must be carefully measured to ensure that the correct amount of each material is sent for mixing.

In modern glassmaking plants the weighing is monitored by a computer, which provides detailed information about the batch mix.

After weighing, the raw materials are fed into 'batch mixers', which operate like large cement mixers and provide a fully mixed batch for melting in the furnace.

Furnaces
The materials used to make a glass-melting furnace must be able to withstand very high temperatures. The lining of the furnace must not contaminate the molten glass in any way, as this would produce flaws in the final product.

There are two main types of furnace in use.

Pot furnace
The pot furnaces used in the early days of the glass industry were mainly coal-fired, and the actual melting took place inside a large fireclay pot. The glassblower would gather the glass from the pot with the end of a long iron pipe, or in some cases with a kind of scoop. He would then pour the liquid into a mould.

Pot furnaces in use today are mainly small-scale and are used for specialized crafts.

Tank furnace
Today, tank furnaces are mainly used for large-scale automated glass production. They give a constant flow of glass to forming machines, and they are usually oil-fired, by burners arranged down each side.

The batch is fed in at one end, and molten glass is removed continuously from the other. Some furnaces can melt over 400 tonnes of glass per day, and are kept in constant operation for periods of up to ten years, after which they must be rebuilt.

After melting, the glass is formed into its final shape by one of many processes.

Working with glass

Each different forming process has a different effect on the glass, and each process therefore has its own specialized use.

Blown
Until the beginning of this century, blowing by mouth was the principal way in which glass was formed (see **Hand-made glass** for description).

The **semi-automatic** method of blowing involves the use of a 'parison' mould into which the molten glass is placed and blown to form the rough shape of the finished article. The parison is then transferred to the blow mould, where it is blown to its final shape.

In the **automatic** forming method the glass is forced down through a hole in an orifice-ring by a large plunger. The glass is then cut into gobs by a pair of shears, and is fed to the automatic machine. The gob drops into the parison mould, is blown to a rough shape, transferred to the blow mould, and blown to the final shape by compressed air. The finished article is then fed into an **annealing lehr** (see page 13), which is like a large oven. In the lehr the glass is reheated and allowed to cool. This has to be done slowly, as when glass is formed, internal stresses are set up. If the stresses were not relieved they would cause the glass to shatter.

Molten glass emerging from the feeder opening. It is cut into short lengths (**gobs**) to form the beginning of a glass container. The gob drops into a mould ready for the next stage (see page 12).

Drawn
Molten glass may also be drawn off from a furnace. Sheet glass is drawn upwards continuously from a tank. The ribbon of glass is started on a metal former known as a 'bait'. The bait is dropped into the molten glass and pulled upwards between rollers. The rollers govern the thickness of the glass. The further apart the rollers are, the thicker the glass becomes.

In **tube drawing** the molten glass flows past a rotating hollow mandrel (a fireclay cylinder). The diameter and thickness of the glass are influenced by air pressure through the mandrel and by the rate of drawing.

Rolled
Molten glass may 'flow' from the furnace continuously between water-cooled rollers. The rollers may be embossed or engraved with a pattern, which is transferred to the surface of the glass. This is known as **rolled figured glass**.

Alternatively, after rolling, the surfaces may be ground down so that they are flat and smooth, to produce plate glass.

Float
In this process, molten glass flows across a bath of molten tin. As the surface of the tin is completely flat and smooth, it transfers smoothly to the surface of the glass.

Extruded
Molten glass may be extruded (forced) from a furnace in the form of blanks. These can later be reheated and pressed into almost any required shape.

Pressed
Pressing is used for objects with a simple basic shape, in which the mouth is wider than the base.

To form the inside of the article, a plunger is used, which pushes the glass against the outer mould.

Cast
Molten glass is poured out and allowed to set in a block. After annealing, to remove stresses, it may be cracked or sawn into small pieces, then ground and polished.

Hand-made glass

Below: This is the layout of a small hand-made glass production line. The men work in teams, sharing the different stages. The master glass worker is responsible for the difficult tasks, such as blowing the glass in the early stages, or making handles. In the background one man is gathering glass from the furnace, while others are blowing or shaping the glass. In the foreground is the 'glory hole', a small furnace where the glass objects are reheated for further working.

Above: Draining a glass furnace. The red-hot molten glass can be seen in the bucket. It has the consistency of hot treacle and a temperature up to 1500°C (3020°F).

Hand-made glass

The earliest small glass bottles were made by the 'sand-core' method. A core of sand or clay was attached to the end of a metal rod and then coated with glass, either by dipping it into a crucible of molten glass or by winding threads of glass around it.

Some time during the 1st century BC a discovery was made in Syria (though we do not know by whom) which was to change glassmaking completely. The metal rod which held the sand core was hollowed out to make it lighter and also to make the heat more bearable. Then a Syrian glassblower blew down the centre of the rod, and so glassblowing was invented.

Glassblowing was the main forming method until the early 1900s, when automatic processes were first developed. Automatic machines now carry out the same functions as the glassblower.

In the hand-blown method, molten glass is gathered from the large melting pot on the end of a hollow blowing iron. After the blower has blown a small 'bubble' inside the glass, the 'gather' of glass is rolled on a smooth slab (marvered). The glass is then blown and shaped by tools, while the blowing iron is constantly rotated to make sure that the shape does not go out of round.

A glassblower carefully blows a piece of glass into shape.

When the base of the article has been shaped, a solid iron rod called the 'pontil' is attached to it with a small amount of molten glass. After reheating in a part of the furnace called the 'glory hole', the top of the article is sheared off and finally shaped. When the article has been completed to the glassblower's satisfaction, the pontil is cracked off, and the article is taken away to the annealing lehr, where all the internal stresses are relieved.

During the working time, the glass is reheated to keep it hot enough to ensure easy working.

A piece of glass is 'marvered' (rolled on a metal slab) to chill the outside so that a skin will form (Stage 3 in the diagram opposite).

A craftsman attaches a 'pontil' to a glass jug for the final stage of shaping. Two people are needed for this (Stage 7).

Making a glass jug by hand

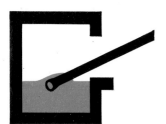

1. Molten glass is gathered from the melting pot on the end of a hollow blowing iron.

2. The blower blows a small 'bubble' inside the glass.

3. The glass is rolled on a smooth iron slab to chill its outside. This is known as 'marvering'.

4. The glass is blown again, this time to a very rough shape of the jug being made.

5. The bowl of the jug is shaped with the aid of a tool.

6. The base of the jug is shaped against a flat plate.

7. The pontil is attached to the base, and the blowing iron is cracked off.

8. The top of the jug is sheared off to the correct height.

9. The shaping of the bowl of the jug is completed.

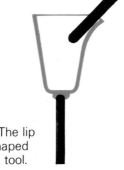

10. The lip is shaped by a tool.

11. A new piece of glass is added to the side of the jug and cut off.

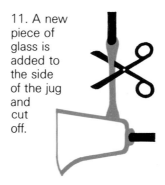

12. The new piece of glass is shaped to become the handle.

The rim of the glass jug is trimmed with a pair of shears (Stage 8).

A piece of glass, which will become the handle of the jug, is attached. Again, the glassblowers work together for this skilled job (Stage 11).

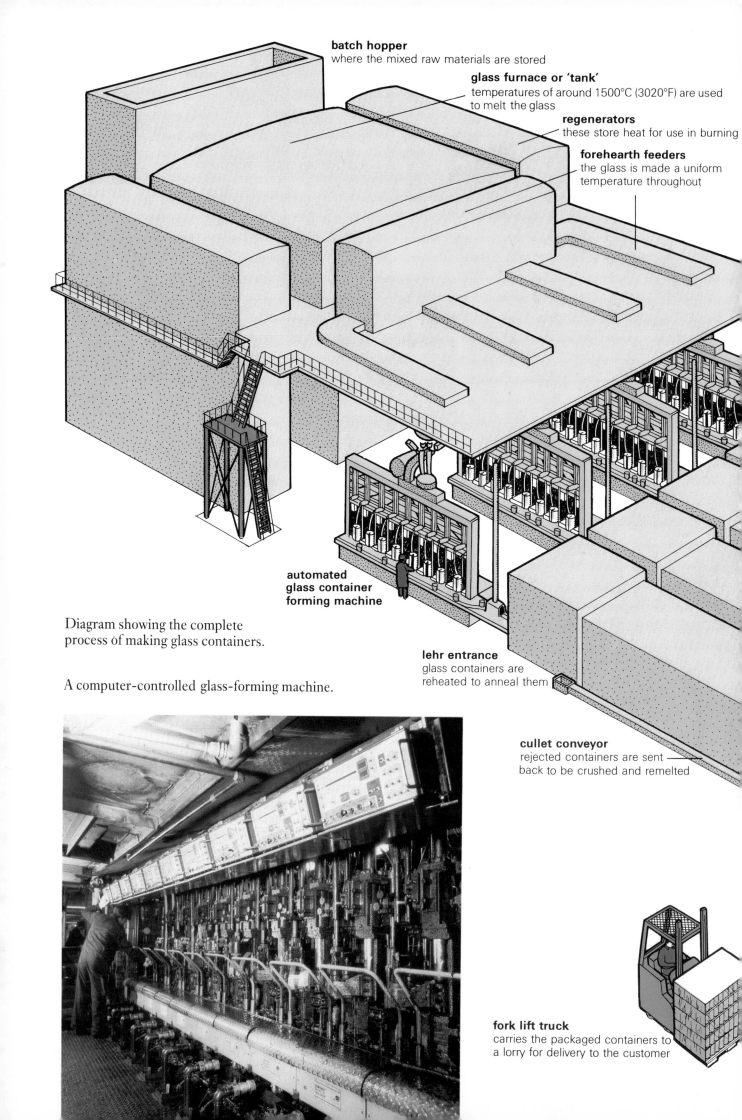

batch hopper
where the mixed raw materials are stored

glass furnace or 'tank'
temperatures of around 1500°C (3020°F) are used to melt the glass

regenerators
these store heat for use in burning

forehearth feeders
the glass is made a uniform temperature throughout

automated glass container forming machine

Diagram showing the complete process of making glass containers.

A computer-controlled glass-forming machine.

lehr entrance
glass containers are reheated to anneal them

cullet conveyor
rejected containers are sent back to be crushed and remelted

fork lift truck
carries the packaged containers to a lorry for delivery to the customer

Making glass containers

Modern-day production of glass containers is a highly mechanised process. First of all the batch (sand, soda-ash, limestone and various additives) are fully weighed and mixed in the **batch plant**. Computers are used to control the plant.

After mixing, the batch is fed into the mouth of a furnace (nowadays usually a tank furnace) and is melted at temperatures of around 1500°C (3020°F). After melting in the furnace, the molten glass moves along a shallow channel called a 'forehearth', where it is conditioned to ensure that at this stage a constant temperature is achieved throughout the glass. Depending on the type of container being made, the temperature may be around 1100°C (2332°F).

After conditioning, the glass is pushed down through an orifice-ring, which is like a bowl with a hole in it. It is then cut into gobs by a pair of shears (like large scissors). The gobs then drop down into the **forming machine**.

The most commonly used forming machine nowadays is the **independent section machine**. This may consist of up to ten sections, working side by side, and two gobs can be made into containers at any one time on each section. Some machines can produce around 140 containers per minute.

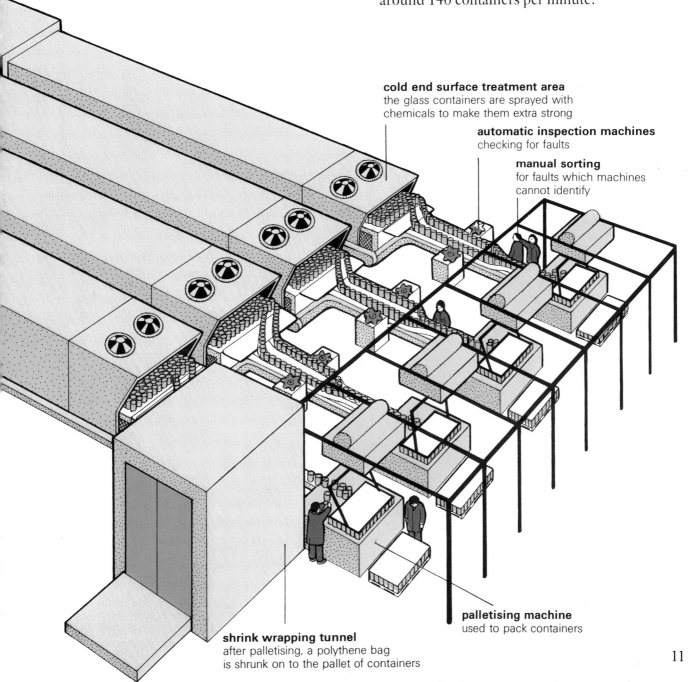

cold end surface treatment area
the glass containers are sprayed with chemicals to make them extra strong

automatic inspection machines
checking for faults

manual sorting
for faults which machines cannot identify

palletising machine
used to pack containers

shrink wrapping tunnel
after palletising, a polythene bag is shrunk on to the pallet of containers

Making glass containers

Two main processes are used on these machines. The **blow and blow method** is used to produce bottles with narrow mouths. The name 'blow and blow' is derived from the fact that the container is blown by compressed air to its rough or 'parison' shape and then finally blown again to the finished article.

The **press and blow method** is used to form containers with wide mouths, such as jars and milk bottles. This process is so called since the glass is pressed into its rough or 'parison' shape by a plunger and then blown by compressed air to its final shape. Both processes are illustrated in the diagram at the foot of the page.

Whichever forming process has been used, the containers are then fed into an annealing lehr. A lehr is a long tunnel through which the containers must slowly pass. It acts as a large oven by reheating the containers and then allowing them to cool slowly. A container may start in the lehr at approximately 540°C (1004°F), and as it moves on the conveyor belt through the lehr, which may be up to 70 feet (21 metres) long, the temperature is gradually reduced.

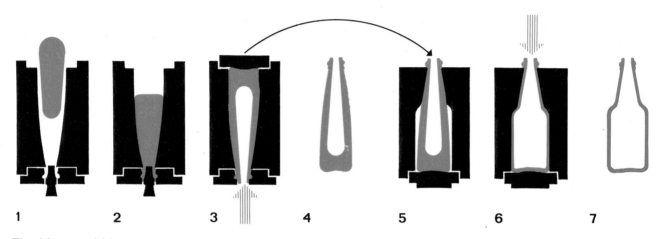

The blow and blow process

1. The gob of glass drops into the blank mould which forms the parison.
2. Compressed air from above pushes the glass down into the blank mould.

3. Compressed air from below blows the glass out against the walls of the blank mould and forms a bubble inside.
4. The parison shape which has been upside down is turned upwards and transferred to the blow mould.

5. The parison settles in the blow mould.
6. Compressed air from above blows the glass out to its final shape.
7. The finished container emerges.

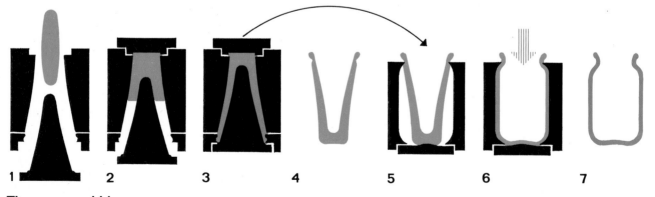

The press and blow process

1. The gob of glass drops into the blank mould.
2. A plunger comes up from below and presses the glass out to the parison shape.

3. The parison is pressed.
4. The parison, which has been upside down, is turned the correct way up and transferred to the blow mould.

5. The parison is positioned inside the blow mould.
6. Compressed air from above blows the parison to its final shape.
7. The finished container emerges.

The reason for putting the containers through the lehr is that glass shrinks on cooling. The outer surfaces shrink more quickly and to a greater extent than the glass contained between them. If nothing was done about this, a great deal of strain would be caused in the container, and the glass would shatter. By slow cooling in the lehr the rate of shrinkage is made the same throughout the glass – thus avoiding cracks.

After annealing, the containers are put through a series of tests to make sure that only high-quality products are sent to the customer.

Two finished glass containers made by the 'press and blow' process are held in 'take-out tongs' before being fed into the **lehr**.

Glass milk bottles leave the lehr after annealing and surface treatment.

The recycling of glass

A very important advantage which glass has over most other materials is that it can be recycled: in other words, it can be used again in the furnace to produce new, good-quality glass.

If you throw an empty bottle or jar into the dustbin you are wasting it. If you put it in a **bottle bank**, it will be taken away to a **glass recycling plant**.

At the recycling plant the glass will be crushed and cleaned, and all bottle tops, caps, and other unwanted items will be removed. Finally it will be fed into the furnace along with the other raw materials for glassmaking.

It takes less energy to melt recycled glass than raw materials.

For every 1 tonne of glass which is recycled, 40 US gallons (182 litres) of fuel oil are saved, which can be used for firing the furnaces.

Play your part in saving energy by saving unwanted glass.

Glass for windows

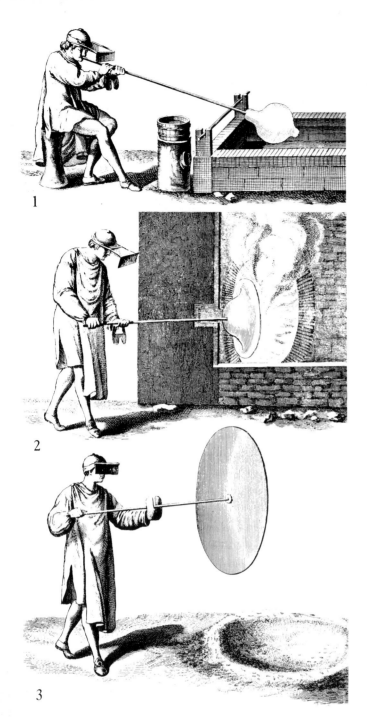

In England the use of window glass dates back to mediaeval times, when, it is thought, some member of the nobility, tired of living in a draughty residence, ordered a local glassblower to find a way of making sheets of glass to cover his windows. The enterprising glassblower gathered some glass on the end of a blowing iron, blew into it, opened up the end of the blown shape with a pair of forceps, and bent the glass outwards. He then spun the blowing iron, causing the glass to rotate outwards, making a larger and thinner circular piece of glass. After cooling, this glass could be cut into sheets. The only piece which was of no use was the middle section where the blowing iron had been attached. The glassblower kept these discarded pieces for his own use.

This is how early window glass was made, and also how the fashion for having a piece of glass with a 'bullseye' began. The effect of rotating the blowing iron produced a piece of glass with circular ridges, which in no way was optically perfect. This type of glass is called **crown glass**.

Cylinder or Broad glass

This method of producing window glass was invented by glassmakers in Bohemia (in Czechoslovakia) and Lorraine (in France). It was achieved by lowering a circular 'bait', or webbed, metal frame, into a pot of molten glass and drawing it upwards. A long vertical cylinder of glass was formed, which was then cut in half lengthways, and flattened out to produce sheets of glass.

Stages in the making of crown glass are shown in these 18th-century engravings.
1. The glassblower blows a piece of glass into shape.
2. The end of the glass 'balloon' is cut open and the lips are peeled back before reheating.
3. After reheating the glass is spun outwards on the blowing iron to form a circular sheet of glass. A 'bullseye' will have been left in the centre, where the blowing iron has been attached.

Bullseyes used to be thrown away, but they are now very fashionable for 'period' windows. They are specially made by hand in the traditional way, for restoration work.

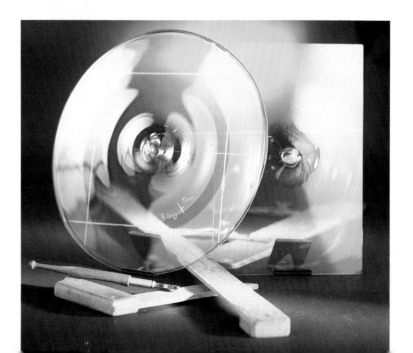

Stained glass

The art of making stained glass windows was developed during the Middle Ages. Its most spectacular use is in the windows of cathedrals and churches.

A stained glass window is made up of thousands of pieces of coloured glass set in a lead framework. First the window has to be designed. The artist begins by drawing a small coloured sketch, and then draws a full-size one, called a 'cartoon', which shows the exact shape, size and colour of the various pieces of coloured glass.

The glass is specially made so that it is uneven in thickness and contains small bubbles and impurities. The varying thicknesses give an interesting variation in colour. The impurities scatter the light and make the glass 'glow'. The colours in the glass are achieved by adding various metal oxides to the batch.

Craftsmen cut the glass to fit the artist's pattern, and the pieces are assembled like a jigsaw puzzle, on a piece of flat glass. The artist then paints details of faces, lines, drapery, etc, on to the glass with coloured enamel paints.

The pieces of painted glass are fired slowly in an oven, so that the enamel fuses with the glass. The pieces are then fitted together in strips of lead to form the complete design.

The dove bearing an olive branch returns to Noah. Part of a stained glass window by Hans Acker, a German glass painter who worked on windows for the Ulm Minster, Germany, in the 15th century.

A skilled craftsman pieces together a stained window and 'welds' the pieces into place by heating the lead framework.

Sheet glass

Sheet glass was first produced around the year 1914. Its two surfaces are hard and shiny, and it is transparent. The main problem with glass produced by this process is that if you look through it at some object, and move the glass up or down, the object will appear to change shape or 'optically distort'.

The raw materials for the glass are melted in a furnace and then the molten glass moves along to the bottom of a **drawing tower**. This is usually 9.5 metres (31 feet) high and the molten glass is drawn up it between rollers. At the foot of the drawing tower the glass temperature is around 950°C (1742°F).

A bait (see page 31) is lowered into the molten glass. The glass clings to the bait and a continuous ribbon of glass is pulled upwards from the furnace. The ribbon is gripped by rough-surfaced, water-cooled rollers at either side of the drawing tower. The rollers prevent the now semi-molten glass from 'waisting' in and losing its ribbon shape. The ribbon is fed up the 9.5-metre (31-foot) high annealing tower between powered rollers which are covered with asbestos to prevent the glass from sticking to the rollers.

The bait is removed at the top of the drawing tower, and the continuous ribbon is cut into required lengths and removed by hydraulic suckers. In the tower the distance between the asbestos-covered rollers determines the thickness of the glass.

The sheet glass process is not widely used nowadays, as the float glass process (pages 18/19) produces glass without optical distortion.

Sheets of glass, cut to size, are handled by automated machinery.

A 'drawing tower' as used in the production of sheet glass.

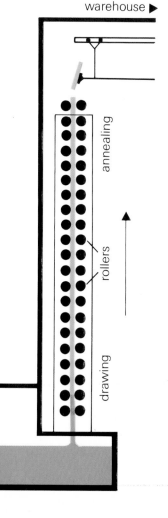

warehouse ▶

annealing

rollers

drawing

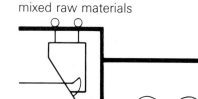

mixed raw materials

molten glass

Plate glass

In the plate glass process, molten glass from the furnace is rolled between rollers in order to make it flat. The contact of the glass with the rollers makes the surfaces dull, so to produce sparkling, as well as flat, surfaces the glass is ground down on large grinding machines. It is then polished to achieve the brilliant, clear quality required of plate glass.

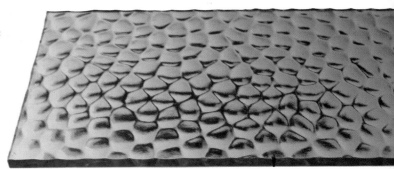

A piece of figured glass.

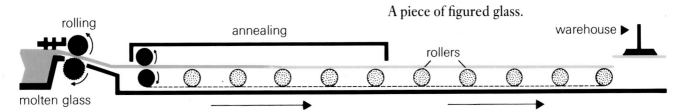

Diagram showing how figured glass is made.

Figured glass

Figured glass is a glass which seems to have a pattern engraved on one of its surfaces. This is achieved by passing molten glass from a furnace between two rollers.

The pattern is engraved or embossed on the surface of one of the rollers, and when it comes into contact with the molten glass the pattern is transferred to the surface of the glass.

This type of glass was invented around 1890.

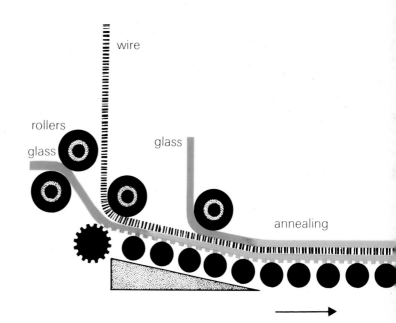

Wired glass

Wire mesh is sandwiched between two layers of glass. In the production process, a 'ribbon' of half the thickness of the final product is rolled, and the wire mesh is laid on top of it. Another ribbon of glass is laid on top of this, and the two thicknesses of glass, with the wire in the middle, fuse or melt together to form one piece of glass.

Clear wired glass is produced by grinding and polishing the top surface and the slightly patterned bottom surface, to make the glass transparent.

Wired glass holds together when broken. Invented in 1895, it was the first safety glass to be made commercially.

Diagram showing how wired glass is made by 'sandwiching' a wire network between two layers of glass.

Wired glass was the first safety glass ever invented and is still in use today.

Float glass

In the float glass process the raw materials for the glass are melted in a furnace at around 1500°C (3020°F) which is fifteen times the temperature needed to boil water.

A thin ribbon of molten glass flows from the furnace into another tank called the **float bath**. The bath is filled with molten tin at a temperature of around 1050°C (1986°F). The glass floats on the surface of the molten tin which, because it is perfectly flat and smooth, transfers to the surface of the glass.

The atmosphere, or air, inside the float bath is controlled, to keep out anything which might discolour or affect the surface of the glass. As the glass moves through the float bath its temperature is lowered to ensure that its bottom surface is hard enough to prevent marking during the next stage of the process. The ribbon of glass is then transported, over rollers, through an annealing lehr, which reheats it and then allows it to cool slowly, avoiding breakage.

When the float glass process was introduced in 1959 it represented seven years of development, a lot of determination and an investment of £7 million (over $10 million). The inventor of the process, Sir Alastair Pilkington, and his development team, recognized the need for a process which could produce a glass of optical accuracy which did not need to be ground flat and smooth.

A view of the glass moving from the float bath to the lehr for annealing.

Molten glass flows from the furnace in a continuous ribbon to float on the surface of liquid tin at a carefully controlled temperature. The brilliant surface makes grinding and polishing unnecessary. After annealing the glass is cut off to required lengths

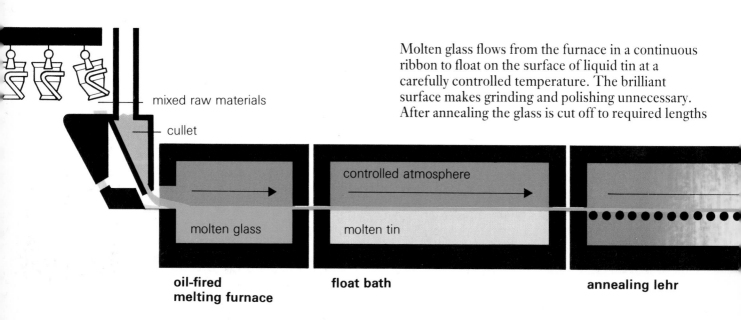

mixed raw materials

cullet

controlled atmosphere

molten glass

molten tin

oil-fired melting furnace

float bath

annealing lehr

Finished sheets of glass made by the float glass process.

After the introduction of float glass a whole new handling process had to be devised. Pilkington Brothers Limited, of St Helens, Lancashire, have therefore developed fully mechanized warehouses which use computers to match orders for a very complex range of sizes and to control cutting so that wastage is reduced.

Float glass has brilliantly smooth, clean and parallel surfaces. It is produced in thicknesses from 2.5 mm (0.1 inch) to 25 mm (1 inch) with no optical distortion.

The automated warehouses are controlled and supervised by skilled operators.

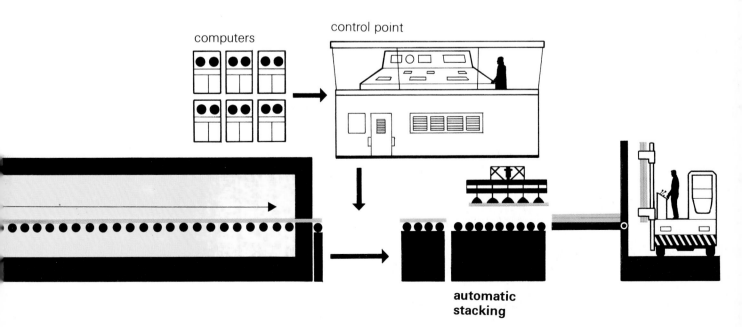

computers

control point

automatic stacking

Glass tubing is drawn off before being cut to length.

Glass tubes

Glass tubing is produced by allowing molten glass to flow down from the furnace past a rotating hollow **mandrel**, which looks like an upside down plunger with a hole drilled through it. Compressed air is blown through the hole, which helps to chill the inside walls of the tubing. The tubing is pulled between a pair of rollers to maintain a constant flow and the same glass thickness throughout the tube.

In a warehouse the tubing is cut to length, and the ends are fire-finished – that is, ground down and polished to give a satisfactory end to the tube.

Light bulbs are inspected on the production line.

Light bulbs

Molten glass flows continuously between water-cooled rollers into a ribbon. The ribbon is carried forward on orifice plates, which are made from a flat metal sheet with round holes cut out of it. The glass is then blown through the orifice plates by compressed air. Under the orifice plates, blow moulds close around the glass shapes which have been formed.

The glass is blown out against the walls of the blow moulds, which open to reveal the final shape of the light bulbs. At this stage the bulbs are still attached to the ribbon of glass. They are then broken off from the ribbon by a rotating disc. Eventually they drop on to a conveyor belt and into an annealing lehr.

A glass fibre mat at the end of the production process, before being rolled and bagged.

Glass fibre

There are two main processes for making glass fibre. In the **crown wool** process, glass flows from the melting tank into a rotating spinner which is perforated with small holes. Because the spinner throws the glass outwards, it is forced through the holes, and emerges as fine glass fibres.

The fibres are sprayed with a binding agent, which is like a kind of glue and which causes the glass fibres to stick together to form a mat as they fall on to a conveyor belt. The mat is 'cured' (a similar process to annealing) in an oven, and is then cut into lengths and rolled into bales.

In the **white wool** process, glass is fed from the melting tank into an electrically-heated platinum crucible (like a large bowl) which has small holes drilled in its base. The glass flows through the holes as fine fibres, and is broken into short lengths by a blast of steam. The fibres drop on to a conveyor and form a glass fibre mat by sticking together. The mat is cured in an oven, and then cut into lengths by a guillotine.

Diagram showing the crown wool process, used in the production of glass fibre mat.

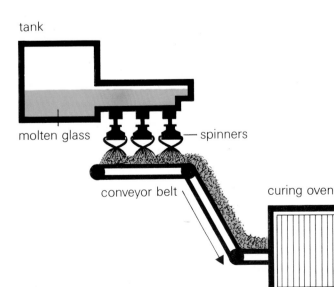

tank

molten glass — spinners

conveyor belt

curing oven

trimmers

slitters
bandsaw

guillotine

rolling machine

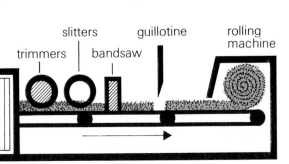

Special kinds of glass

Glass is not just used for everyday items such as windows and bottles and jars. One of its very special uses is for the lenses of spectacles and cameras. This type is called **optical glass** and must contain no faults whatsoever.

When it has been melted in the furnace the bubble-free glass may be cast into blocks, rolled into sheets or extruded into bars. After careful annealing it may be further processed by remoulding, grinding and polishing.

Another special use for glass is in **car windscreens**. Most new cars have laminated windscreens which do not disintegrate into hundreds of tiny pieces when they are broken, as they used to when they were made of 'toughened glass'.

Laminated glass is produced by 'sandwiching' a sheet of clear plastic between two sheets of glass. The glass is held together by the plastic, which prevents shattering.

Another special use for glass is in **laboratory glassware**. Test-tubes, beakers, and equipment of all shapes and sizes must be able to withstand high temperatures and must not break on cooling. Pieces of tubing and rods are reheated over a burner and reshaped with special tools. Complicated pieces of laboratory glassware are made in separate sections and 'welded' together by heating.

Glass is used for drainage pipes beneath London's Barbican Centre.

A vacuum flask is made of two glass containers, one inside the other. The neck end is sealed, the inside surfaces are silvered, and air is removed from between the two containers to create a vacuum. It is then sealed at the bottom end. The photograph shows the glass containers ready to be silvered.

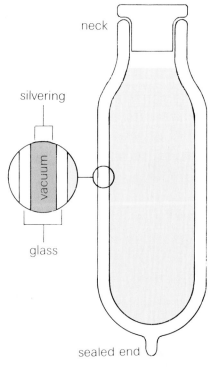

neck

silvering

vacuum

glass

sealed end

New uses

One of the latest developments in glass is the use of **optical fibres** in telecommunications. The fibres are very fine, high-quality strands of glass through which light rays can travel. The ray of light is transmitted at one end of the fibre and bounces along the fibre length, to be received at the other.

Optical fibres can be used to carry signals in the same way as telephone wires, which are made from copper and known as co-axial cable. An optical fibre is very thin and lightweight and can carry around 1,000 telephone calls more than copper wire: which means that many more optical fibres can be included in a large multi-wire cable.

The signals transmitted by optical fibres are much stronger than signals transmitted by copper wire. Therefore they do not need as many repeaters (boosters) to help the signals to travel over long distances.

Unlike ordinary copper cable, optical fibres do not suffer from radio interference. It is also impossible to 'tap' telephone calls (by using a listening device) on optical fibre cables.

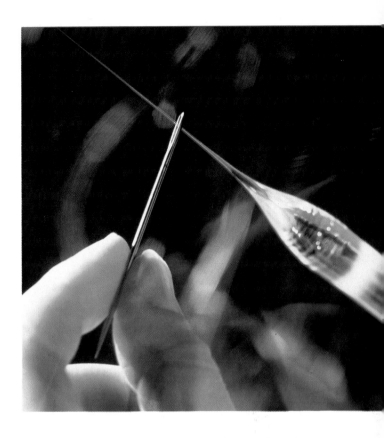

Glass rods are heated and stretched to produce long, thin optical fibres. The size of the final fibre is shown by the needle.

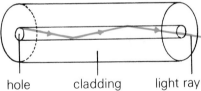

hole   cladding   light ray

A light ray 'bounces' along a length of optical fibre; it can also go round corners. Information is coded into digital pulses which pass down the fibre as bursts of light.

The process for heating and stretching glass rods is difficult and requires precision as well as the highest quality of glass.

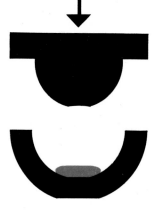
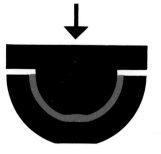

molten glass drops
into the mould

a plunger moves down
on top of the glass

the glass is pressed
into the shape of the mould

the final shaped glass
container emerges

Pressed glass objects. Decoration can be
part of the mould or plunger, and will be
on the inside or outside surface of the glass
object.

Decorating glass

Much of the glassware which we use around the
house has been decorated in some way or
another. A vase may have a faint floral
decoration; a bowl may have a criss-cross pattern
on it; or a drinking glass may have rings 'painted'
around it.

Pressed

Simple objects such as ashtrays or glass plates
may be patterned at the same time as they are
being formed. The mould is engraved, by
machine tools, with a design; the molten glass is
pressed into the mould; and the finished article
emerges with the glass shaped into a raised
pattern made by the engraved mould.

Engraved

Glass bowls, jugs or goblets may be engraved by
hand. A design is marked on to the surface of the
glass in wax crayon. The glass is held against an
abrasive wheel which cuts out the entire design.
Designs can be very complicated, and great skill
is necessary at the cutting stage.

A decoration may be 'deep-cut' by holding the
glass against the upper edge of an abrasive wheel.
Or it may be 'intaglio', cut by holding it against
the lower edge of the wheel; this produces a
much lighter form of decoration.

An even finer decoration is produced by holding
the glass against the lower edge of a copper wheel
on to which a fine abrasive liquid is fed.

Fine engraving can be applied to
glass, using a power tool with a
fine abrasive tip.

Glass plates and bowls are masked before sand-blasting. This photograph and the ones below were taken at The Glasshouse, Covent Garden, London, a workshop where glassblowers can be seen at work, and where their finished pieces are exhibited.

Below: A glassblower wraps a piece of molten coloured glass around the other glass on her blowing iron. Below right: After blowing, the coloured glass has fused with the clear glass to produce a streaky effect, similar to that found in marbles. The glassblower trims the glass with a pair of shears to make a bowl.

Sand blasted

A very difficult form of decoration is produced by sand blasting.

The design to be transferred to the glass is cut out of a 'mask' (like a stencil) which is then taped to the surface of the glass. A gun which fires thousands of small sand particles by compressed air is used to blast the surface of the glass, producing a frosted appearance in the areas which have been cut out of the mask, and leaving the rest of the surface smooth. Some lovely designs are produced in this way.

Etched

This is a way of producing yet another style of decoration. The design is cut into the glass as in the engraving process. The areas which are not to be etched are then covered with wax, and hydrofluoric acid is applied to the cut surface. As the acid eats into the glass it etches the design, producing a frosted appearance.

Fusing

The fusing of different colours can produce some spectacular effects. A piece of molten, clear glass is formed to its eventual shape, and strands of different-coloured glass are stuck to its surface. The glass is then reheated, and the coloured glasses fuse or melt into the surface, producing a streaky, or rainbow, effect.

A handful of marbles – just a drop in the ocean of millions produced each year by Marble King Inc, in the United States.

Red-hot glass is cut into small cubes which drop into the shaping machine. This machine has moving rollers which give the marbles their round shape.

Using glass

Marbles

People have been playing marbles for hundreds of years. The first 'marbles' were probably round pebbles, but in the 1700s true marble, with its 'veins' and interesting colours, was first used.

Today, most marbles are made from glass. They may be plain, transparent, or brightly decorated, with names such as 'glassies', 'cat's eyes' and 'rainbows'.

Glass marbles are made by melting sand, soda-ash and limestone with recycled glass called 'cullet'. The molten glass is formed into small cubes, which are then ground down between revolving abrasive wheels which remove the corners and make them perfectly round. Any extra decoration is put inside the marble when the molten glass is formed into its cube shape.

Some marble manufacturers such as Marble King in the USA can make as many as 220 marbles a minute.

Paperweights

Paperweights may be plain or beautifully decorated pieces of glass. They are generally made by hand, and demand a great deal of skill.

A 'gather' of molten glass is taken from a furnace on the end of a rod. It is then shaped, either with special tools or in a mould. While the glass is still very hot, small pieces of coloured glass, such as studs or small flowers, are pushed into the bottom surface of the glass, and another piece of molten glass is stuck to them. With reheating the glasses fuse together, and colours are spread through them, making a charmingly patterned paperweight.

These tiny rods of glass, which look like candy-sweets and seaside rock, will become part of a paperweight (shown in the photograph on the right). They are formed into a pattern and covered with a large blob of clear or coloured glass. The glass is then ground and polished, and acts as a magnifying glass over the decorative design inside.

Lampworking

Lampworking is a method of forming shapes in glass. It, too, takes years of practice on the part of the lampworker. Skilled craftsmen can make animals, birds, trees and various other shapes.

Glass rods are heated in a flame until they become soft and workable. The lampworker can then pull the rods apart to make thin strands, or he can bend the glass into almost any shape he wishes. By 'welding' together pieces of glass the lampworker may create a tree with several small birds sitting in it, or a life-like horse.

Enamelling

In this ancient craft an artist, using **enamel** paint, decorates the surface of a glass goblet, jug or plate. Afterwards the article is fed into an oven where the heat causes the enamel to fuse on to the surface of the glass, and the colours become hard and fast.

Nowadays enamelling is used on milk bottles as a way of advertising cornflakes or toothpaste, or the name of the dairy where the milk came from. The work is done by an enamelling machine which can produce a design in up to three colours. For each colour a silk screen is made with areas cut out of it to allow the enamel paint to reach the surface of the glass in exactly the correct places.

Another kind of enamelling is **Cloisonné** which was developed by the Chinese during the Ming Dynasty in the 16th century. The western name is derived from the French word 'cloison', meaning a cell. A design is created by soldering copper wires on to a metal base to create cells. The cells are then filled with coloured enamel pastes and fired. The surface is polished and the wires are gilded.

Making a decorative glass animal. The horn of a unicorn is added in white glass to the blue 'horse'. All that is needed for this job are pieces of glass, a small flame, patience and skill.

The craftsman paints the design on to the glass. The enamel paint is a mixture of oxides and oil. When fired in an oven the oil burns away and the oxide is fused on to the surface as a hard and permanent design.

All kinds of glass

Bottles and jars

Large quantities of bottles and jars are needed, so they must be cheap to produce. They must also be able to withstand bumping together on filling lines, which work at a very high speed.

Bottles and jars are made from soda-lime-silica glass and are mostly formed on automatic bottlemaking machines which have speeds of up to 140 bottles per minute.

Flat glass

Glass used for windows and doors must be perfectly clear and must have no optical distortion. It must also be able to stand up to hard use.

Flat glass is made from soda-lime-silica glass and is formed by drawing, rolling, polishing, and the float glass process.

Domestic glass

Domestic glass (for everyday drinking, storing of liquids, etc) must look good and must be very clear. It must also be able to stand up to constant use. The glass must not affect the taste of its contents in any way.

Normal domestic glassware is made from soda-lime-silica glass. It can be formed by mouth blowing, automatic blowing, or by hand and automatic pressing.

Domestic lead crystal glass

Lead crystal has a sparkling finish which looks very attractive. It gives a clear ringing sound when tapped (lightly!) with a pencil. As it is comparatively soft it is also easily cut and polished.

Lead crystal is made from lead glass and is mouth-blown or hand-pressed, depending on the article being made.

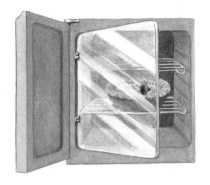

Ovenware glass

Glass for ovenware must be able to withstand high temperatures and also frequent heating up and cooling down. The glass must also be able to withstand scratching from knives and forks. Pyrex is an example of this type of glass.

This type of glass is borosilicate which is pressed into the shape of plates and dishes in a mould and then annealed very carefully. The glass can be decorated by enamelling.

Thermometer tubing

This glass must be able to stand heat and cold and must also be transparent.

Some tubes are made from soda-lime-silica glass, some from borosilicate, and others from lead crystal, depending on the temperatures to be measured. The tubes are usually formed by automatic and hand drawing.

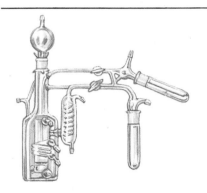

Laboratory glassware

This glass must be resistant to chemicals. It must also be able to withstand heat.

It is made from borosilicate glass by lampworking, by mouth and automatic blowing, and by hand and automatic pressing.

Chemical glassware

Chemical glassware must not be affected by, and must not affect, chemicals. It must be strong enough to carry dangerous liquids safely. It must be clear, so that liquids can be seen. It must withstand high temperatures and immersion in water after heating.

It is made from borosilicate glass in tube lengths. The tubes are reheated and bent into shape.

Glass fibre

Glass fibre must be strong; it must not be affected by corrosive substances; and it must be able to withstand high temperatures.

It is made from soda-lime-silica glass by the white wool and crown processes.

Collecting

Bottles

Bottles which were made in the early 1700s are collectors' items and today are worth a lot of money, but you needn't go as far back as 1700 to find interesting shapes, designs and colours. Bottles vary in size from about 1.2 metres (4 feet) to around 25 mms (1 inch) high.

Collecting enamelled milk bottles can be fun in itself since there are thousands of different designs enamelled on them.

Light bulbs

Some people collect light bulbs, and it is surprising to discover how many different sizes, shapes and colours there are. To prove it, just look around your own house.

To start a collection all you have to do is wait until a bulb stops working and ask for it.

Wrap your glass collection in tissue paper and store it in a box full of polystyrene chips. You will find that it will last longer this way.

Whatever you do with glass – be careful! It could break and cut you. Handle with care.

Milk bottles have undergone several changes of shape over the years. They have also lost weight – from 19ozs (539grms) to 6ozs (170grms).

Who works in a glass factory?

Batch controllers

Operate computers which measure the amounts of raw materials to be used.

Furnacemen

Control the temperature of the furnace and sort out any problems which affect the molten glass.

Machine operators

Operate the bottlemaking machines, lubricating the mould equipment when necessary.

Glassblowers

The craftsmen who make bottles and glass ornaments with a blowing iron.

Lehr controllers

Control the speed, temperature and annealing problems associated with a lehr.

Sorters

Remove any bad quality glass at the cold end of the process.

Maintenance workers

Fitters and engineers who carry out repairs on the process and mould equipment.

Management and secretarial staff

Make business decisions on a day-to-day basis concerning the running of the processes.

Glossary

Annealing   The process which prevents glass from shattering after it has been formed. The outer surfaces of glass shrink faster than the glass between the surfaces, causing strain which can lead to shattering. By reheating the glass and allowing it to cool slowly this can be avoided.

Bait   A webbed metal frame used to draw molten glass.

Batch   The mixed raw materials which are used to make glass.

Boric oxide   A compound used in making borosilicate glass.

Bullseye   The round, whorl shape in the centre of old panes of glass.

Calcium oxide   A compound used in glassmaking, which comes from lime.

Co-axial cable   Copper cable used to transmit signals.

Coolant   A liquid for cooling down engineering work. Usually water.

Crown glass   The old-fashioned method of making window glass.

Crown wool   A process used in making glass fibre.

Crucible   A ceramic or clay bowl.

Crystalline   Resembling small crystals, or crystal shaped.

Cullet   Recycled or waste glass.

Curing   Similar to annealing.

Drawing tower   Used in the sheet glass process for drawing molten glass.

Enamel   A soft glass compound of flint or sand, soda potash and red lead.

Extruded   Forced through a die or continuous mould for shaping.

Feeder   The part of the furnace which ensures that the glass has a consistent temperature throughout.

Float   A method of producing high quality window glass.

Fluxes   Oxides used to produce glass which is easy and inexpensive to shape.

Forehearth   An extension of the furnace, where glass is made at the same temperature throughout.

Forming   Shaping, or moulding into shape.

Gather   A small amount of glass taken from a melting pot.

Glazes   A hard-fired glass finish on pottery.

Glory hole   An opening in a small furnace used to reheat glass articles.

Gobs   Short lengths into which glass is cut for forming.

Intaglio   A light engraving on the surface of glass.

Lehr   Similar to an oven, used for reheating glass and allowing it to cool slowly.

Mandrel   A forming or shaping tool used to make glass tubing.

Manganese   A metal powder used as a flux in glassmaking.

Marver   To roll molten glass on an iron slab.

Orifice-ring   Bowl-shaped, with a hole in the bottom.

Parison   The rough shape of a glass item. It is sometimes known as a 'blank'.

Pontil   A metal rod, to which a glass article is attached.

Potash   Potassium oxide (a flux).

Pot furnace   A pot-shaped furnace made of clay.

Pyrex   Trade name for borosilicate glass.

Sand core   A shape made from sand, around which strands of molten glass are wound.

Selenium   A metal powder used as a flux in glassmaking.

Silica   A type of sand derived from minerals such as quartz.

Soda ash (sodium oxide)   A flux used in glassmaking.

Supercooled   Frozen into shape.

Tank   A glass furnace.

Tube drawing   Drawing glass tubing into shape.

Waisting   Glass narrowing in the middle.

White wool   A process used in making glass fibre.

Index

Acknowledgements

Threshold Books and the publishers gratefully acknowledge the help given by Pilkington Brothers plc, United Glass Containers, and by Glass Bulbs Ltd, in the production of this book.

Illustration credits

Photographs: Ann Ronan Picture Library page 5 (top); British Telecom 23 (top, bottom left); Geoffrey Drury 3 (bottom), 4 (glass ship made by Lichfield Glass Sculptures, City of Lichfield, Stafford, UK), 7, 8 (taken at Dartington Glass Ltd, Torrington, Devon, UK), 9 (bottom left and right), 17, 20 (top), and 24, 25 (taken at The Glasshouse, Covent Garden, London), 26 (bottom right), 27 (top), 27 (bottom left; paperweight made by Paul Ysart); Glass Manufacturers Federation 30; Arthur Lockwood 14 (top); Marble King Inc, USA (photo Chet Hawes) 26 (top and bottom left); Pilkington Brothers plc 14 (bottom), 18, 19, 21; Schott-UK/Geoff Price 15 (bottom), 16 (top); Schott Glaswerke, West Germany 22 (top); Sonia Halliday Photographs 15 (top); Tony Stone Associates 2; Thermos Ltd 22 (bottom); Thorn-EMI 20 (bottom); Trustees of the British Museum 3 (top); United Glass 6, 10.

Diagrams and drawings: Ray Burrows pages 10, 11, 16, 17, 18, 19, 21; Gillian Newing 5, 9, 12, 22, 23, 24; Carole Vincer 28, 29. Diagrams are adapted from information in *Making Glass* published by the Glass Manufacturers Federation, and from information supplied by Pilkington Brothers plc, St Helens, Lancashire.

First published in 1985
by Faber and Faber Limited,
3 Queen Square, London WC1N 3AU

Typeset by Phoenix Photosetting, Chatham, Kent
Origination by Culver Graphics, London
Printed and bound in Belgium by
Henri Proost & Cie PVBA
All rights reserved
© Threshold Books Limited, 1985

The How It Is Made series was conceived, designed and produced by
Threshold Books Limited,
661 Fulham Road, London SW6 5PZ

General Editor: Barbara Cooper

British Library Cataloguing in Publication Data

Paterson, Alan J.
   Glass.—(How it is made)
   1. Glass—Juvenile literature
   I. Glass   II. Series
   666′.1   TP857.3

   ISBN 0–571–13411–4